# THE AFFIRMATION STATION

## DAILY AFFIRMATIONS AND JOURNAL

### TANIA JOY ANTONIO

#### ILLUSTRATED BY MARTINA DI RUSCIO

Balboa Press books may be ordered through booksellers or by contacting:

Balboa Press
A Division of Hay House
1663 Liberty Drive
Bloomington, IN 47403
www.balboapress.com
1 (877) 407-4847

ISBN: 978-1-5043-4260-5 (sc)
ISBN: 978-1-5043-4261-2 (e)

Library of Congress Control Number: 2015916729

Print information available on the last page.

Balboa Press rev. date: 02/05/2016

BALBOA
PRESS
A DIVISION OF HAY HOUSE

INSPIRED BY AND DEDICATED TO MY PRECIOUS DAUGHTER GEMMA-LOVE.

I AM FOREVER GRATEFUL TO YOU FOR CHOOSING
ME TO BE YOUR MAMA XO.

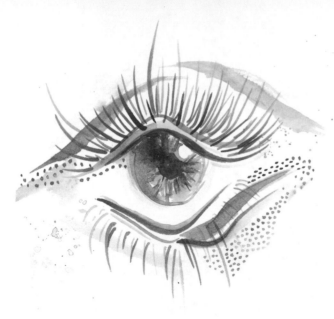

I AM LOVE.

I AM LOVE. YOU ARE LOVE.

LOVE IS YOU. LOVE IS ME.

LOVE IS SO LOVELY, WOULDN'T YOU AGREE ?????

# I AM HAPPY.

EACH MORNING WHEN I WAKE,

HAPPINESS IS A CHOICE I MAKE.

I AM HEALTHY.

I MAKE HEALTHY CHOICES THAT ARE GOOD FOR MY BODY, MIND AND SOUL.

THEY MAKE ME FEEL GOOD. THEY MAKE ME FEEL WHOLE.

# I AM KIND.

I AM KIND TO MYSELF AND KIND TO OTHERS.

WE ARE ONE, SISTERS AND BROTHERS.

# I AM POSITIVE.

Positive Vibes

OPEN HEART.

OPEN MIND.

POSITIVE THOUGHTS.

POSITIVE VIBES.

# I AM STRONG.

STRONG MIND.

STRONG HEART.

DEEP WITHIN IS WHERE IT STARTS.

# I AM CALM.

LET'S BE CALM AND MEDITATE. IT FEELS SO GOOD, DON'T HESITATE.

BREATHE IN DEEP, NICE AND SLOW.
FEEL AT EASE AND GO WITH THE FLOW.

I AM A
DREAMER.

WHEN I GROW UP, I WANT TO
BE ME.

PASSIONATE... AUTHENTIC...

WILD AND FREE.

# I AM PEACE.

LOVE AND PEACE IS WHO WE ARE.

SPREAD IT ALL AROUND, NEAR AND FAR.

# I AM BLESSED.

WITH MY HEART WIDE OPEN

I KNOW THAT ALL AROUND,

WITH EACH NEW DAY

THERE ARE BLESSINGS TO BE FOUND.

# I AM FREE TO BE ME.

BE PROUD OF WHO WHO WHO

YOU ARE.

YOU ARE A UNIQUE AND BRIGHT SHINING STAR.

# I AM GRATEFUL.

I START EACH DAY WITH AN ATTITUDE OF GRATITUDE.

A GRATEFUL HEART IS WHERE IT STARTS.

I AM ONE WITH THE EARTH.

BARE FEET PLANTED ON THE GROUND,

ENJOYING ALL OF NATURE'S SOUNDS.

THE ANIMALS, THE TREES, THE SUN, MOON AND RAIN;

I LOVE THEM ALL, JUST THE SAME.

I AM A MIRACLE.

I AM A MIRACLE MADE WITH LOVE,

A DIVINE BLESSING FROM ABOVE.

# I AM BE**YOU**TIFUL.

BEAUTY REFLECTS FROM THE

INSIDE OUT. A KIND HEART AND

SOUL IS WHAT IT'S ALL ABOUT.

BELIEVE IN MYSELF,

IT'S WHAT I MUST DO.

SET MY GOALS

AND FOLLOW THROUGH.

# JOURNAL

A PLACE FOR YOU TO EXPRESS YOURSELF... ... ... ... ... ... ...

LET IT ALL OUT.
JUST BE TRUE.
TO THE ONE AND ONLY
AUTHENTIC YOU.

I AM _____

I AM _____

I AM _____

I AM _____

I AM _____

I AM _____

I AM _____

I AM _____

I AM _____

I AM _____

I AM _____

I AM _____

I AM _____

I AM _____

I AM _____

I AM _____

I AM _____

I AM _____

I AM _____

I AM _____

I AM _____

I AM _____

I AM _____

I AM _____

I AM _____

I AM _____

I AM _____

I AM _____

I AM _____

I AM _____

I AM GRATEFUL _____

I AM GRATEFUL _____

I AM GRATEFUL _____

I AM GRATEFUL _____

I AM GRATEFUL _____

I AM GRATEFUL _____

I AM GRATEFUL _____

I AM GRATEFUL _____

I AM GRATEFUL _____

I AM GRATEFUL _____

I AM GRATEFUL _____

I AM GRATEFUL _____

I AM GRATEFUL _____

I AM GRATEFUL _____

I AM GRATEFUL _____

I AM GRATEFUL _____

I AM GRATEFUL _____

I AM GRATEFUL _____

I AM GRATEFUL _____

I AM GRATEFUL _____

I AM GRATEFUL _____

I AM GRATEFUL _____

I AM GRATEFUL _____

I AM GRATEFUL _____

I AM GRATEFUL _____

I AM GRATEFUL _____

I AM GRATEFUL _____

I AM GRATEFUL _____

I AM GRATEFUL _____

I AM GRATEFUL _____

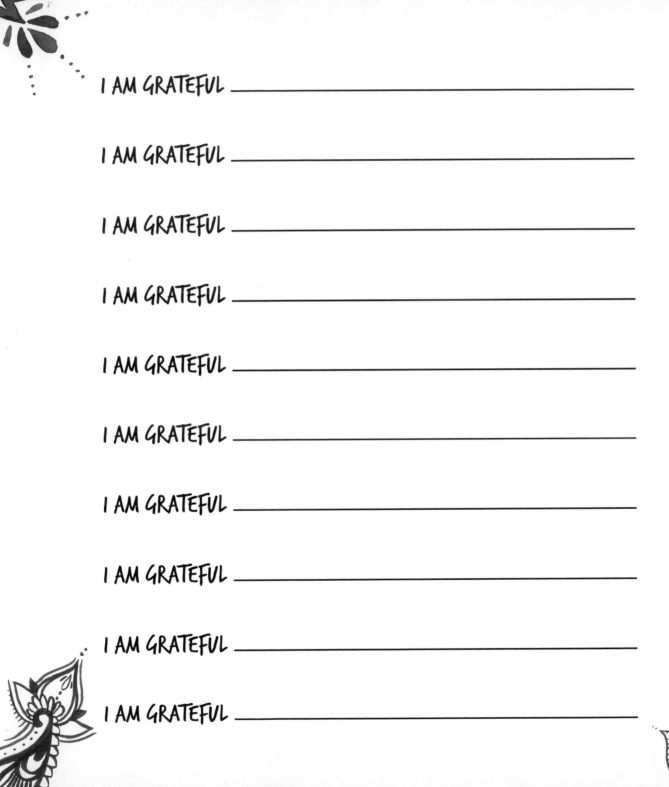

# ABOUT THE AUTHOR

Daughter, Wife, super blessed to be a Mother. Entrepreneur. I am a dreamer. I believe in the power of positive thinking, self-love and creating a life that feels good on the inside. Living from a place of Love and Compassion. I believe with passion, purpose and persistence we can manifest our dreams. I believe gratitude is the best attitude. Vision Boards, Flower Crowns, Meditating, Journal keeping, Fitness for the Body, Mind and Soul; these are a few of my favourite things.

Printed in the United States
By Bookmasters